Meditation

The Definitive Practical Manual For Meditating To Unleash
The Power Of The Mind

(The Stunning Advantages Of Mediation)

Kennith Donovan

TABLE OF CONTENT

The Matter Of Consciousness 1
The Philosophy Of Meditation 18
Taking Control Of The Day 53
Vasudhaiva Kutumbakam ! 66
How To Meditate 80
The Issue Presented By Mindlessness 88
The Influence Of Presence 91
Relaxation And Calmness-Inducing Breathing Techniques 95
The Union Of Peace And Understanding 106
Meditation Practice Everyday 111
Including A Mantra In One's Breathing 135
Our Programming 140
There Are No Mishaps 146

The Matter Of Consciousness

Consciousness consists of the presence of thought, a chemical reaction, or cerebral robotics. As our body is an advanced and complex structure, so is the intellect, which serves as its operating system. The brain is an autonomous self-operating system that operates in a cycle, with information serving as its command. In turn, the information has an effect on the existing information. An action occurs when a strong desire or fear is present; without these desires or fears, which are embedded in the brain through information, the mind cannot function. The mind has a preference for delight over suffering. Therefore, the mind attempts to occupy its software with pleasure-related knowledge or data. The information that something is more likely to cause pain is the result of a large delight in the anticipating mind. So enlightened are attempting to control their lives in accordance with mental processes.

Every material process contains conscious awareness.

Form vs formless.

Formless is also called counsciousness. And form is recognized as the substance of consciousness.

Space is the closest manifestation of formlessness.

Does thought have or lack form?

What would you call the information on the hard drive that the computer is displaying at our command? The answer can be found in the scientific concept of pn junction. Diode , A science candidate will readily comprehend the operation of a junction. How a signal is transmitted to a junction or didode to achieve the desired result. Consequently, electric impulse is the manifestation of a shape. Similarly, the radiance of the sun. It consists of particles. Depending on the instrument used to observe it, it sometimes behaves as a particle and sometimes as a wave. If we gaze at something with our eyes, we will see images, and if we listen to its vibrations, we will hear sounds. The wall next to you will appear as a wave when viewed through an x-ray machine.

So, whether it is a wave or an electric impulse, everything takes shape.

Thus, our thought is a form as well.

The closest example of formlessness, according to the majority of individuals, is space. If this is the case, then why cannot time be formless? Okay????

Thus, the correct response is "Time is a theory, a concept." There is no time apart from change. Change exists, but not time. We allocated time for calculations. to quantify the objects and events. Consequently, if time does not exist, how can it be shapeless? Consequently, the possibility of time travel is ruled out by this statement. Temporal travel is impossible.

However, space exists, and everything exists in space. But if we query . Which comes first, Gyata or Space?

Form can occupy space, and its energy can traverse space. So that form may traverse space. Space is ubiquitous. However, what if we are unaware of space? The sciences discuss a unified realm in space. What is this constant, unitary, or point-like field? Space cannot be gyata, and the experiencer of void in profound slumber when the body's (i.e., the mind's) desires do not function is gyata or the unified field described by science.

In this case, the smallest particle is a single point field, also known as gyata in the Vedas. This field is itself contentious.

The subsequent section will focus on consciousness or Gyata. And sound of Gyata, Sound Meditation, and a great deal more.

Please refer to my book "Reality of life" by Aniket Vats for additional information until I finish the next section.

Metta Meditation

Metta is synonymous with compassion or benevolence. Metta meditation, also known as loving-kindness meditation, is a modern technique of meditation that aims to help you become more kind to yourself. Sometimes you become anxious because you are overly critical of yourself and your responsibilities. However, if you begin to be kinder and more considerate to yourself, you can manage your stress levels. Other benefits of this form of meditation include the development of positive emotions, an increase in self-acceptance, and a more compassionate disposition.

To employ this meditation method:

1. Settle into the location you have designated for meditation.

2.Recline in comfort and close your eyes.

3.Begin by cultivating compassion and benevolence for oneself. Wish yourself pleasure and the best of luck.

4.Move on to other individuals, such as a friend, a "neutral" person, then a difficult person, and ultimately the universe.

In addition to meditation, relaxation is an excellent way to combat stress and anxiety. This topic will be expanded upon in the subsequent chapter.

Relaxation Techniques

By increasing your level of concentration and awareness, relaxation techniques allow you to refocus your attention away from your anxiety-inducing stressors and onto something soothing. This is a more advanced type of mindful meditation. Here are some relaxation techniques you can employ to help you relax:

Automatic Calmness

Autogenic refers to something that originates from within. In autogenic relaxation, you combine body awareness and visual imagery to effectively combat stress and anxiety. Here are the procedures to follow:

•Repeat suggestions or words in your mind to help you unwind and alleviate the muscle tension you experience.

•Imagine a tranquil environment and concentrate on regulating your respiration and slowing your heart rate.

•Notice the various physical sensations in your muscles, and conclude by imagining each leg and arm in succession.

Progressive Relaxation of Muscle

Focus on tensing and relaxing each group of muscles in order to practice progressive muscle relaxation. Here are the procedures to follow:

•Begin by contracting and relaxing the muscles in your ankles, then work your way up to your feet, legs, knees, arms, chest, neck, and head. You may also choose to commence with your neck and cranium and work your way down to your extremities.

•Tense your muscles for approximately five seconds, and then relax them for thirty seconds. You can repeat this a number of times to relieve any tension in your body.

Create gorgeous and tranquil mental images of placid and soothing situations and locations using mental imagery or visualization. Here are some measures to take:

•Sit in a tranquil location, close your eyes, adjust your clothing if it is too restrictive,

and concentrate on your respiration.
•Incorporate as many senses as possible, including sight, scent, touch, and sound.Consider the sound of the rising and falling waves, the scent and flavor of the briny water, and the warmth of the sun on your exposed skin if you envision yourself unwinding in an ocean-like setting.

After practicing these relaxation techniques, you should feel calm and at ease.

In this instant, when I was completely sober for the first time in years, I realized that things would never improve unless I took action. I was forced to endure this. This has been the lesson I've had to learn for eons. No external factor can provide enduring happiness. Before learning this lesson, I realized I would never progress. I stepped out of the victim role for the first time and accepted that everything that has ever occurred to me was the result of my own decisions, my own construction. The entire state of disorder was an illusion. For despite appearances, there was no such thing as coincidence, and as it turns out, none of my enemies are stronger than I am. As a result, I realized that if I could conquer myself, I could accomplish anything. With my life in shambles all around me, I realized I needed all the assistance I could get to even have a chance this time around.

Thus, I again knelt before the earth and prayed. Three times striking the ground with my fist, I cried out to God for assistance. God, the most misused and abused word in the English language, made it abundantly obvious that I had to assist myself. As unique manifestations of the divine, we are each endowed with an abundance of spiritual abilities and privileges that few individuals ever recognize. I resolved, moving forward, to realize these talents and use everything I possessed to serve the greater benefit of all humanity. In utter submission, paradoxically, one attains the utmost authority. As with all things, this surrender can only occur in the eternal present moment and sometimes must occur moment by moment.

Although initially agonizing, the years that followed were nothing short of miraculous. Statistically, there is a ten-to-one chance that someone with my form of addiction will receive the necessary treatment. 10 percent or less of those who receive treatment survive the first year of recovery. I now understand that these statistics are deceptive. I now realize there is a superior, simpler method to escape this torment.

I realized that everything was dependent on my level of consciousness. Therefore, I endeavored to release attachments and increase my level of consciousness. This occurred several years ago, and my accomplishment along the way has been astounding. Doors have opened precisely when they should have. My fortunes began to improve. I rebuilt my life, followed the synchronicities, and had a succession of profound spiritual awakenings that shattered my mind and obliterated all the illusory conceptions I had been taught to believe about God and the nature of reality while growing up.

So many of us reared in the west are indoctrinated with belief systems that are incomplete. I soon began to have all of these profoundly physical and profoundly transformative mystical experiences. It was as if my body were filled with light, vitality, and euphoria. I quickly realized that I was not the only one waking up. It appears that humanity as a whole is awakening, and our greatest days as a species lie ahead. We are all in this together, and the present moment is crucial. We must recognize who we are and come together.

This book is filled with numerous treasures. These are sacred Truths that I have uncovered as a result of extensive research prompted by my quest to overcome addiction, discover the Truth, and maintain an elevated state of consciousness, always endeavoring to assist others and serve the Creator in any way possible. I set a goal for myself to comprehend what "enlightenment" meant and achieve it. Today, in 2021, I am still sober and filled with pleasure and optimism. My life has become extraordinary, and I am here to share my happiness and inspire others to have faith! Within each and every one of us is a Higher Power fervently desiring to manifest in our lives and bless us with a life beyond our highest imaginings. Now more than ever, tapping into this higher power is crucial for every human being.

Changing our individual selves and allowing this greater identity to manifest in our lives is the most essential thing we can do right now to change the world for every person on the planet. By altering our interior world, the external world faithfully follows suit. Because the outer world is a reflection of the interior world, this is the case. "As within, so without." Consequently, if you raise your level of consciousness, it will have a profound effect on those around you and reverberate into the global mind in order to raise the collective consciousness at this crucial time. As stated, your level of cognizance governs every aspect of your life. Spiritual searchers today have numerous advantages that did not exist in previous generations. The level of consciousness on the planet is rising, making it simpler for the individual to raise his or her own level of consciousness, and a vast array of social services, welfare, and health care are accessible to anyone in need. Ancient esoteric knowledge that was once restricted to specific regions of the world and only accessible to spiritual pilgrims who had to travel to distant lands is now available to us all online. In the west, our material requirements are essentially met. In addition, we have an infinite selection of entertainment and diversions. Materialism has been beneficial to us. However, it is evident that something is absent.

This lacking component is obvious to everyone. It is as readily available as the tip of your nostril. Simply practice turning inward is all that is required.

The Philosophy Of Meditation

Meditators have been extolling the benefits of meditation for centuries. Some consider meditation to be a mystic experience, making it difficult to articulate. They claim that you will continue to experience these benefits long after the sessions have concluded. It is said that meditation expands your senses beyond the five senses.

You can sense yourself, connect with your inner self, and derive genuine pleasure from within, independent of other people or external objects. Researchers have attempted to elucidate the science of meditation due to the unusual and exceptional nature of its benefits. Their findings explain why seating alone can facilitate healing, authentic pleasure, and even the resolution of other complex challenges.

Nevertheless, despite the fact that these researchers are diverse and employ diverse methods, they all concur that meditation is real and that its benefits are real. According to these researchers, through a process known as neuroplasticity, you can use meditation to alter your mind's structure, strengthen your immune system, improve your well-being, alter your thoughts, increase your gray matter, combat depression, reduce stress, integrate your various body parts, and reduce mental distractions.

Alterations in the brain

According to neuroscientists, meditation strengthens the connections between the brain's cells, making the brain healthier and more effective. Another study revealed that continuous meditators have higher levels of gyrification. As a result, they are able to assimilate information more quickly, making them quick learners with enhanced memory and comprehension. According to numerous studies, meditation induces beneficial brain alterations in the individual.

Another 2009 study demonstrated that meditation is associated with the growth of gray matter in the brain. Scientists hypothesize that the increased development of gray matter is responsible for enhanced affective, cognitive, and immune responses. Since gray matter is essential to the development of the central nervous system, it is hypothesized that it promotes positive emotions, improved behavior, and enhanced emotional stability.

To gain a clearer understanding of how meditators can accomplish all these benefits, scientists have investigated meditation's mode of operation. Meditation appears to affect more than just the chemical and physical components of the brain. Neuroscientists demonstrate that meditation also affects the various brain functions. This indicates that meditation can delay some parts of the brain while speeding up others, for example, meditation is associated with decreased connectivity and network activity. These two functions are associated with disorders such as anxiety and actions such as inattention.

Health Advantages

On the other hand, physicians and researchers have primarily focused on meditation's health-related benefits, as opposed to the neurocognitive benefits emphasized by many of the studies described above. For instance, it has been discovered that meditation improves one's memory capacity. In 2011, researchers examined explicitly concentrated attention meditation practitioners. Within three months, the meditators were meditating for over five hours per day. After the period, the participants' ability to sustain voluntary attention was evaluated and found to have improved.

Different research suggests that meditation is analogous to a muscle; it can be strengthened and enhanced by meditating more. It makes no difference whether you meditate for five hours, twenty minutes, or even ten minutes. Studies indicate that even if you only meditate for 10 minutes, you will begin to experience the benefits of reduced tension, enhanced contemplative and mindful thought, sustained attention, enhanced memory, and resolution of depression.

Even after eight weeks of meditation sessions, you will be able to reduce your tension levels, according to the most recent research on meditation. According to test results, meditators performed better on stressful multitasking assessments. Scientists explain this using cortisol, a stress hormone whose levels were discovered to decrease following meditation. If you meditate prior to engaging in a distressing activity, you will find that your tension levels decrease during the activity.

Scientists explain that to get the most out of meditation, one must be aware of what they are doing, what they wish to accomplish, and how meditation will help them accomplish these goals. Whoever meditates without knowing what to expect is merely exercising. The greatest comprehension of meditation can be attained by recognizing the brain's function in the practice. By knowing how meditation affects chemical, physical, and mental processes, one can comprehend the significance of silence, stillness, and proper posture.

Developing An Alternative Routine And Finding Time For Meditation

Do any of the following topics resonate with you?

That you have begun meditating, but you are having trouble finding the time?

You intend to begin your meditation sessions, but you are uncertain if you will have the time? Or That you began meditating but halted because you did not have enough time? If you answered yes to any of these questions, this chapter has something for you.

Time is currently one of the greatest challenges confronting meditators. It is possible to be so occupied that the only leisure you have at home is to slumber. However, some individuals use time as an excuse for their inability to meditate. It is even amusing that sometimes you know you are lying to yourself about being occupied, but you continue to use time as an excuse in order to feel justified.

While you have time to refresh Instagram for the twentieth time, you have also updated your Facebook profile five times, and you have a 30-minute delay button on your alarm clock. Didn't you? In that case, you are making an excuse based on time.

Even if your schedule is so full that you rarely have spare time, this should not prevent you from meditating. Therefore, once you resolve to meditate, allow nothing to stand in your way. Did you know that you can meditate while waiting for a train or bus, while stuck in traffic, while having a shower, or even while sitting on a park bench? If you rarely have leisure at home, you should not give up on meditating. You can practice meditation anywhere and at any time.

Meditation regimen

Experienced meditators advise that regular meditation practice is optimal. Similarly to how we are accustomed to eating breakfast in the morning, lunch at midday, and dinner in the evening, meditators benefit from the same pattern. Create time in the morning, shortly after waking up, if possible. This will provide you with pleasure, relaxation, and vitality throughout the day. When you establish a regimen, your body becomes so accustomed to the program that you will notice the difference whenever you neglect a session.

How to carve out time for meditation

The following advice will assist you in incorporating meditation into your daily regimen.

Profit from both day and night

If you cannot find time to meditate during the day, arise up early in the morning and meditate, or meditate before bed to help you unwind.

Establish objectives for each session, and record them in your calendar.

When a meditator ties their sessions to specific goals, it becomes easier to adhere to the regimen and track progress, according to research. Possible objectives for a session include relaxation, temper management, health improvement, and mental enhancement.

Inform a close friend of your plans.

If you are having difficulty meditating, ask a close friend to encourage you to persevere. It could be your spouse, a romantic partner, or a guardian. By telling them about your program, they will constantly remind you, ask you if you completed it, and when you may be tempted to skip sessions, they can serve as a source of motivation and encouragement.

Choose a meditation area

If you can meditate at home, designate a space with a comfortable chair, flower vase, incense, candle, and carpet. As soon as you make the location sacred to you, it will serve as the most effective reminder.

Timing your schedule

Sometimes you must simply test yourself to determine whether you have sufficient time. By evaluating your schedule, you can determine where you can fit in meditation time.

Additionally, you will be able to ask yourself the following:

- How long do I typically sleep? Are there excessive quantities?

- How long do I view movie series and television programs?

- How much time have I spent socializing with my pals?

- How many hours exist between the time I awaken and the time I report to work?

- Do I ignore my alarm clock?

By answering the following questions, you can determine whether you are using time as an excuse.

Seize every moment of freedom

If you do not have enough time, you can still meditate, albeit in an atypical location and at odd hours.

- If you have a one-hour lunch break, you can still meditate prior to dining. • If you are immediately leaving work and have to commute, take 10 minutes to meditate before you arrive at home. • If you work in an open office space, inform your coworkers so they will respect your stillness.

Finally, there is no point at which time will be sufficient. You will never know how an hour passes because you will always hear your inner voice instructing you to unwind a little bit. Therefore, when you begin to meditate, time will continue to appear as an obstacle. Everyone can meditate, regardless of whether they have a fixed schedule or free time. Sessions do not have to last 20 minutes; sessions as brief as five minutes can be effective. Also, it is not necessary to meditate at home, so you can meditate whenever and wherever you like.

Choose an everyday item that you sometimes misplace, such as a key, cell phone, pen, headwear, toothbrush, or remote control for your television.

Now, actively try to lose this item. Hide it well and attempt to forget where you hid it.

You will likely not be able to lose this object, despite your efforts, because you have focused a great deal of concentration on the process of losing it and attempting to forget. At this juncture, it is virtually unthinkable to lose it. Why do you believe this?

You will never lose a dependency, behavior, thought pattern, addiction, or any other detrimental propensity if you employ a great deal of thought, attention, focus, conflict, and effort. It will be present in some form for a very long time, perhaps indefinitely. The point is that whatever you consistently focus on will be difficult to abandon. This is the reason why people who complain frequently are never satisfied: they can't stop thinking about and focusing on the issues they're complaining about. Eventually, the problems become an intimate part of their existence. Remember that rival adversaries maintain a strong bond.

Do not consider the midlife crisis; do not resist, struggle, or oppose it. Let it be lost by being forgotten.

*Fifteen minutes of silence and deliberate respiration. Repetition of the mantra: "I need not hang on. I permit it to be lost.

(Share this experience with the hashtag #30DaysLose)

Day 18

Exercise:

Repeat the words "Guilt", "Shame", and "Regret" ten times aloud. Do not hurry. Between each iteration, pause. You are free to take a long inhale during the interval. You may keep your eyes open or closed. Again, repeat the words slowly and observe any internal thoughts, feelings, or images that arise.

Now, repeat these words 10 times while smiling.

What meaningless credence we accord words like Guilt, Shame, and Regret. We use these words on ourselves and others; they become part of our internal voices' regular vocabulary. In the end, they are nothing more than meaningless phrases. What would these words be without a facial expression, tone, emphasis, or inflection?

When you uttered these three specific words, what thoughts did you have, how did you feel, and did your body react? People tend to interpret a reaction, such as shortness of breath or a frown, as melancholy; however, this is a learned behavior. We have been instructed to feel and think a certain way about remorse, humiliation, and regret. The truth is that these terms have no meaning.

As with most negative thoughts and emotions, a midlife crisis thrives on these three words and the taught responses they elicit. But recognize them for what they are: meaningless terms.

*Fifteen minutes of silence and deliberate respiration. The mantra is: "I am not Guilt, Shame, or Regret."

(Share this experience with the hashtag #30DaysGSR)

Chapter Two: Feelings!

A

Are you unhappy, regretful, or depressed? You're not going insane, and you're not lacking as a rational human being; you're perfectly normal. These emotions serve a physiological purpose: they inform us when we've done something incorrect. If this natural defense mechanism were removed, a person would not be able to learn from their errors because they wouldn't realize anything was amiss.

Can you calm your mind despite the stress of work? This is one of the queries you should instead ask yourself.

The symptoms of a life lived against nature are fervor, anxiety, and dread. They are anomalous impulses, as opposed to sentiments, that stem from an individual's best interests and noblest capacities and accurate perceptions of things. Because of this, we should endeavor to eradicate fervor, anxiety, and dread from our lives. So, if every time you deceive, that sensation of foreboding disappears, can you truly claim that life is better because you feel less threatened?

For centuries, philosophers and psychologists have debated emotions. One school of thought holds that emotions are the result of mental processes, while the other contends that they are inherent human characteristics. Others contend that emotion is simply a byproduct of our brain's rational processes, whereas some believe that emotion has evolved to aid in our survival. There may never be a definitive answer, but discussing emotions is nonetheless enthralling.

Stoic philosophers believe that emotions are neither good nor evil in and of themselves, but rather result from a misinterpretation of the situation. This aspect is essential to comprehend because, by internalizing the emotions that result from a lack of complete comprehension, we can rationally choose our response to the situation and act accordingly. For instance, if you are hungry and someone tells you to buy a cake from them, but you are ten minutes away from home where a delicious salad is waiting for you, your emotional response to the hunger – such as fear that you will be late for dinner or frustration at the discomfort of hunger – may influence your decision to purchase the cake. This leaves you with less money and a likely surplus of calories and deficiency of nutrients. In contrast, if you had acted rationally, you would have chosen to go home and prepare the salad, knowing that you could endure the inconvenience of hunger and that it would be less expensive and healthier than the cake.

People experience emotions as negative or positive based on their circumstances; however, Stoics believe that emotions are inherently impartial and are either positive or negative based on our interpretation of them.

Consider the emotion that we all share: wrath. This emotion is distinguished by the frequency with which it occurs in your daily life. Anger can be beautiful, as when you stand up for the oppressed, desirable, as when it motivates you to complete a difficult project, and dangerous, as when it causes you to swerve in front of someone else's car. A person who consistently makes decisions based on wrath and their emotions in general is not Stoic. Remember that the solution to mental stability in life is not to suppress emotions, but to redirect them.

Philosophers have been investigating wrath since antiquity. Aristotle famously wrote that the powerful should not express wrath, but if necessary, they are justified in using it as a form of punishment. Seneca, a Stoic philosopher, argued that wrath is a "temporary madness" whose sole purpose is to cause harm to others. To live a joyful existence, according to the Stoics, one must learn to exert maximum control over one's emotions.

Fear is another emotion that can be irrational when associated with particular situations, individuals, objects, or environments. Some people develop so many phobias that they develop a social anxiety disorder; those who experience this type of dread wish to avoid social interaction for the rest of their lives.

Stoicism can be employed to manage the ups and downs of daily existence. However, it is not suitable for all individuals. A Stoic will feel good about unfavorable events that occur in his or her life because he or she will consider emotional development at that time. Possibly the most difficult emotion for someone who does not practice Stoicism to comprehend is happiness.

Rather than averting emotion wholly, Stoic philosophy encourages us to deal with all emotions wisely and constructively, transforming a potentially detrimental stimulus into a growth-promoting opportunity."

The Practice of Conduct

Ancient Stoics studied desiring or wishing; how to wish effectively. According to their reasoning, one's desire or wish for what is correct seems natural. By extension, we will desire and wish well for everyone (Aristotle believed that even evil individuals shared this disposition). The most practical step was convincing others to want something you knew they would want if you simply explained its benefits, as this serves as a stepping stone toward your eventual desire for it.

One of the fundamental precepts of Stoicism is that humans should have disciplined self-control over their emotions so that they can concentrate on what is most important: the desire to assist others. Seneca developed the Stoic Disciplines of Desire, Action, and Assent. The Discipline of Action is one of these three. This one is concerned with philanthropy and accepting one's fate; a Stoic's aim is to wish others well with the understanding that other people's actions are beyond their control and are therefore predetermined by destiny.

This philosophical practice is neither complicated nor profoundly personal. Stoicism aims to help you regulate negative emotions, such as wrath, fear, anxiety, and envy, through rational rather than volitional means. The Stoics emphasize reason as the primary foundation of human conduct, in stark contrast to its major rivals (Plato emphasized emotion (especially love), most clearly embodied by his concept of eros, and Aristotle theorized that virtue is founded on the habit of performing all actions well). Stoics defined virtue not in terms of external conquests or material achievements, but as an internal state that can be attained through practical wisdom, living an ethical life, and self-discipline.

Instead of simply instructing you what to do, this book will elucidate the approaches through modern science-based self-tests that assess your emotional depth.

Chapter 1 of Marcus Aurelius is devoted to his introduction. Meditations is one of the most influential texts ever written on Stoicism. In it, he advises against responding to anger with more anger: "If you are angry, be assured that the thing that made you angry will not make you less angry." Instead, he recommends practicing compassion for those who have wronged us: "You are no different from them; you, too, have offended others in various ways. You may avoid making certain errors, but the thought and inclination remain."

At first inspection, this may appear to be an odd doctrine, as many psychological models advocate taking time away from our problems or resolving them through confrontation. However, when we practice mindfulness and cultivate self-compassion instead of harshly condemning ourselves and making unfavorable comparisons between ourselves and others to justify our wrath, we can achieve genuine contentment regardless.

In addition, it has been demonstrated that attempting alternative methods to control wrath is highly beneficial, and that the key to any Stoic principle is to control your emotions. For instance, you may employ Mental Distancing.

Mental Distancing

You can use this technique to help yourself calm down when you are feeling angry. It is a coping skill that many psychologists recommend as an alternative to repressing your emotions or lashing out at the source of your displeasure, both of which can result in regret and long-term harm.

Mental distancing entails placing mental distance between yourself and the source of your rage, allowing yourself a brief reprieve from feeling furious by temporarily removing it from your presence.

Follow these steps:

Focus on inhaling in through your nostril and out through your pursed lips as you take three full breaths.

Imagine something that brings you happiness. This does not have to be a physical object; it could be anything, such as listening to a favored song or perusing a favorite book.

When you feel calmer, visualize the source of your wrath while simultaneously holding an image of something that brings you pleasure.

Another method for regulating interior emotions is to learn not to fixate over external factors. Remind yourself that there are aspects of your life over which you have no control, such as a person's height, paralysis, voice quality, autism, and many others. Meditation can be a beneficial instrument when it comes to these kinds of disciplines.

Premeditatio Malorum

One of the most well-known Stoic exercises is premeditatio malorum, which translates to "the pre-meditation of evils." Seneca describes this exercise as follows: "A man should not fear death, but he should fear never beginning to live" (Letters, 6). The purpose of the exercise is to prepare you for challenging situations. When faced with a challenging circumstance, it can be very difficult to maintain emotional control. This meditation may help you cope with them more effectively.

The Stoics advocated routinely visualizing the worst-case scenario for any given situation. According to Stoics, these activities are a part of the discipline of living.

The exercise involves visualizing a situation in which you must confront your worst anxieties and preparing for it. Imagine, for example, that you have been gravely offended by someone and you feel compelled to respond emotionally to them. Ask yourself the following questions to complete this exercise: 1) What if I lost control of myself? What could occur? 2) What if things got even worse? 3) What if I never lose control and instead maintain it?

The purpose of these queries is to convince you that whatever transpires may be for the best. If you lose control, there may be adverse outcomes. However, if you maintain your composure, you may also achieve a favorable outcome. The crucial point is that even if the worst-case scenario occurs, things may still turn out well.

In this exercise, it is extremely important that you truly imagine all those negative outcomes as vividly as possible. This exercise will only work if you do it regularly over a period of time, at least once a week. It is not meant to make you feel fear and anxiety but to prepare yourself in advance for difficult situations. Therefore, it is important to imagine all the possible negative outcomes in detail and with an open mind.

[VM15]The Stoic Happiness Triangle

We all want to be happy. We have been conditioned from birth with the knowledge that happiness is an intrinsic human desire and a fundamental part of life. However, what may not be as apparent are the steps one must take to achieve this goal. The Stoic Triangle of Happiness holds the key to a good, happy life by cultivating an excellent mental state.

First things first: acknowledging what makes us unhappy and avoiding these things actually helps us create lasting happiness.

Second, we need to practice mindfulness; living in the present moment without judgment or criticism of ourselves or others will allow us to sense more fulfillment in our lives. It will also enable us to remain calm during adversity.

Last, you should develop your emotional resilience by cultivating positive thoughts about yourself and others.

Stoicism ultimately aims to enable anyone to be happy, to have eudaimonia – life-fulfillment. This Greek work encapsulates the ideal Stoic kind of satisfaction. It is the bliss one feels when they are on their deathbed, think back over their life, and comment, "I have had a decent life!" To the Stoics, eudaimonia is an absolute satisfaction one could accomplish.

In Stoicism, happiness – eudaimonia – depends upon three elements:

Control

Responsibility

Virtue

Control: The Stoic partitions the world by a rule called the polarity of control into equal parts. It says that there are things in this world that we can control, such as our judgment, motivation, wants, and expectations. All else lies outside our ability to control, like others' assessments of you, your body, notoriety, material belongings. The division of control causes us to complain and suffer less and keep up our composure more. The Stoics encourage us to focus on and improve at the things we can control and let go of things we cannot.

Responsibility: The Stoics require us to assume responsibility for all that transpires within our control, without accusing others. What use is accusing another? Stoicism believes the best in people and that no one consciously acts at the villain of their own tale. So, if someone injures you, they likely did it through obliviousness or because they believed it the best judgment. When we assume responsibility for things and decide to react to them with intelligence and judgment, we become more reasonable and autonomous — liberating us from mental subjugation to other people.

Virtue: Righteousness is the foundation of Stoic bliss. To accomplish eudaimonia, they encourage us to practice the four cardinal virtues – prudence, justice, fortitude, temperance. These will come up at various points further on in this book.

These three factors form the foundation for happiness within Stoicism.

Taking Control Of The Day

Why Controlling Your Day Is So Important

Do you wish to achieve big accomplishments with tremendous success? In this circumstance, "mastering your day" is essential.

It does not matter how you spend your time as long as you are not deliberately attempting to live a chaotic existence.

The professional, personal, and physical aspects of my existence were, to say the least, beyond my control. One day, my business instructor approached me and inquired about the activities I had engaged in the previous day. She was informed that I was "all over the place." I attempted to recall specific accomplishments from the previous day, but came up barren. Or week. a week or month in duration. I squandered months of my existence wandering aimlessly and concentrating on nothing in particular because I never focused on the day.

I was trapped in a cycle and experiencing some sort of despondency, and I had no idea how to escape.

She gave me sound advice by stating, "You must take charge of your day if you wish to regain control." Unfortunately, it took me a few years before I began to pay heed to her advice.

In a relatively brief period of time, you can go from being in a dire situation to having total control over your day. However, you must make an effort on purpose. When you begin to give each day the attention it deserves, you will be able to begin stepping into your grandeur and working toward the realization of your personal life vision.

To help you take charge of your day, I will share seven strategies with you today.

Tips for Making the Most of Your Day

1. Know precisely what you want to accomplish by the end of the day – To take charge of your day, you must approach it with the intent of attaining your objectives and realizing your personal life vision. If you do not have a clear concept of what you want to accomplish during the day, it will be very simple for you to spend the time aimlessly wandering around with no sense of direction.

Establish Precise Objectives After determining what you wish to accomplish, the next stage is to determine the daily actions that must be performed in order to reach your goals. Having well-defined objectives enables you to map out a path from where you are now to where you envision yourself in the future.

3. Create a Plan of Action - After establishing your objectives, the next stage is to determine how you will achieve them. Whether your goals are biennial, monthly, or even weekly, you must follow a specific process and execute specific actions in order to reach your destination. These actions will constitute your strategy. To have total control over your day, you must first be aware of the daily tasks that you must perform.

4. Schedule It in Your Calendar - My business coach would frequently tell me, "If it's not on your calendar, it doesn't happen." My life has revolved around my calendar for the past 24 years, which I associate with being active, having meetings, being away from home, attending conferences and seminars, traveling, making hotel reservations, scheduling appointments, and experiencing tension. I avoided scheduling anything because I resented the factors that

contributed to my exhaustion, which was caused by my schedule. You will have more control over your day – and your life – once you begin scheduling the actions necessary to reach your objectives on your calendar.

5. Achieve Precise Accuracy in Your Objectives "Follow One Course Until Successful" is Robert Kiyosaki's recommendation when discussing the relationship between concentration and success. Create a plan of action, then implement it and schedule its execution. After that, you should focus on the actual exccution. Each day, I must record the "Daily Big Three" duties because my planner includes this feature. My action plan, objectives, and overarching objective are interconnected in some fashion. These three focal points assist me in maintaining concentration.

The key to successfully navigating change is to devote all of your time and energy to creating the new, rather than fighting the old. ~Socrates

Develop Useful Habits – It is merely a habit if you are "Floundering around," lounging on the settee, wandering aimlessly, and telling yourself you are trapped. Develop beneficial routines. I developed these habits before my life began to spiral out of control. These are genuinely terrible patterns! As a result, I ended up going in the exact opposite direction of what I had intended. In order to get off the sofa and move around, it will be necessary to modify one's behaviors. I decided to begin taking 10,000-step morning treks to establish a new regimen that would entail increasing my physical activity. I continued doing this for 117 consecutive days! This resulted in the formation of a new routine and habit, as well as the elimination of an undesirable routine and lack of routine. If you develop a series of effective behaviors, you will achieve success. You establish consistency and routine in your existence.

7. Keep track of your progress. Mastering Your Day is not a vague concept founded on sentiments or emotions. If you have specific objectives and a daily plan of action, you will be able to monitor your progress and determine how much you have accomplished. Always keep track of your finances. This allows you to determine if your strategy is successful, as well as what should be modified or adjusted accordingly. If it is not measured, then it cannot be improved.

Today, start taking control of your day.

To achieve your goals successfully, you must have complete control over each day. To achieve anything of significance in life requires self-discipline, deliberate action, and undivided focus. If you establish habits that are complementary to your action plan, you will ultimately reach a point where some of your actions will feel as though they are being performed automatically. But to get there in the first place, you must initiate action.

It is said that the first stride of a thousand-mile voyage is the most difficult. Tradition Chinese Knowledge

Taking charge of your day begins with directing a single moment as to how it should proceed. You have the ability to determine how you employ your time and whether it is working for or against you. You, your grandeur, your objectives, and your life's vision are all factors that make it worthwhile to exert effort to master each day.

Making your meditation practice a routine

In order to see consistent benefits from your meditation practice, you must transform it into a consistent daily habit, and one way to do this is to simply set a quantity of daily meditation time.

For instance, your minimum meditation time could be at least 10 minutes in the morning and at least 10 minutes in the evening; this could be your minimum quota for meditation. In this way, you actually have a sort of minimum thing to do, and when you feel like it, or some days or most days, it is entirely up to you, you may want to meditate for 20 to 30 minutes.

Depending on the day, the minimum time requirement could be as low as 10 minutes.

Additionally, you can use a variety of apps for monitoring your habits, and there are a variety of apps for tracking habits and recording how many minutes you have spent working on a particular habit.

In addition, writing down the number of minutes you meditated per day can be extremely motivating, as you can then see your progress and realize that you have meditated for 30 or 60 minutes per day, respectively.

You simply enter this information into your app, and it will display the total number of hours that you have meditated in the past week, month, year, and for your entire existence. This can be very motivating to see how much you are progressing with your meditation practice.

Additionally, you can record every day in a journal or similar document how your meditation practice is benefiting you or affecting you in any manner.

Simply jotting it down may give you something to reflect back on, and it may also be motivational if you see a variety of benefits.

And you can simply record all the different effects you've observed as a result of your meditation, such as increased self-awareness, forbearance, calmness, comfort, stress resistance, and so on.

So you simply record anything that effects your feelings or that you believe may be a result of your meditation practice and observe how it affects you.

Summary

In conclusion, I strongly recommend that you consider making meditation a daily habit, that you do it consistently, and that you do it for at least three months in order to transform your meditation practice into a consistent habit.

Thus, you will likely have built up a great deal of momentum, making it simpler to continue your meditation practice and to experience a variety of consistent benefits as well.

Hence, this is yet another reason why I strongly advise you to contemplate daily meditation.

Vasudhaiva Kutumbakam !

There is no such thing as a local occurrence; every occurrence is universal. There is no such thing as an isolated location; every location is a portion of the universe. Every living and nonliving object exists within the universe. When you assist a person, you indirectly help the universe, and when you damage someone, you are inevitably injuring the universe in some manner. Each and every thought you have has some effect on the universe. Similar to how trillions of cells make up the human body and remain an integral part of it, the universe is composed of trillions of living and nonliving objects. An injury to one part of the body causes pain throughout the entire body, and healing that injury would alleviate this pain. Similarly, when you harm another person, you are truly injuring yourself as well, as you are also harming the universe, of which you are a part.

So, Vasudhaiva kutumbakam - the world is one family entails that we are all a part of the same universe, because we all live in this universe, and therefore we are all connected or related in some way, either directly or indirectly, because we are composed of the same five elements - Earth, water, fire, air, and ether - that make up the universe. We all support and abide by our respective family members in both good and poor times because there is an emotive bond between us and a sense of mutual obligations. However, when it comes to anything outside the family, we adopt an ostrich-like attitude, becoming indifferent, apathetic, and even hostile, without realizing the true meaning of family or extended family - Vasudeva kutumbakam.

Similar to how every rupee of profit or loss you generate individually becomes a part of your organization's profit or loss and eventually reflects in the balance sheet and determines your own bonus and increments, every good or bad action we take individually will collectively reflect in the universe's balance sheet. Global warming, the economic downturn, and terrorism are a few examples. Few individuals are responsible for these extreme occurrences, but the entire world will be affected by them.

Therefore, we must remember that every thought and action we have has an effect on the universe, and that individual actions have a cumulative effect on everyone's existence. This is why we say that when you aid a person in need, someday when you are in need, assistance will come to you in some other way through another person, as the universe returns the favor you have done to it.

Hope that people will comprehend the true meaning of this great divine phrase "Vasudhaiva Kutumbakam"; the day this occurs, the world will be a better place to live, full of love, compassion, brotherhood, mutual respect, and cooperation, etc.

Every residence is a part of a society, every village or town is a part of a state, and every state combined constitutes a country. An invisible bacterium, no matter how small, is a vital part of the human body and has the potential to save or destroy it. Similarly, every being, whether living or non-living, human or otherwise, is an important and essential part of this one world, the universe in general, and is therefore connected in some manner.

Therefore, every event, no matter how large or small, and every being, whether significant or not, affects the world constantly through their thoughts and actions. Global warming affects all living things, and recession and war have affected all nations. If we can connect the connections and see the big picture, we will realize that we all belong to the same family.

The effects of Biden's election as U.S. president, Terrorism, Modi's demonetization and GST, the Corona Virus, Russia's invasion of Ukraine, and other events are not limited to the U.S., Syria, Iraq, Russia, Ukraine, and India. We live in a world that is more interconnected than ever before. Every nation's survival depends on the resources and actions of other nations. India could have surpassed China if Pakistan had not existed. The invention of computers and information technology by Americans has enabled millions of Indians establish a strong foothold in the United States and around the globe. Yoga practice has assisted millions of westerners in regaining serenity and tranquility in their lives.

Every particle of water eventually reaches the ocean. Clouds produced in one region of the globe cause precipitation in another region. We consume food and other necessities produced by others in other regions of the world. Migration occurs between continents. One sun grants vitality to every living thing on the planet. It is the same group of nine or ten planets that determine the fate of everyone on Earth. Every human being is comprised of the same five elements (Earth, water, fire, air, and space) known as the Panchamahabutas. Our diet, our use of natural resources, and our physiology are identical. How then could we possibly not be interconnected in some way?

Every individual's thoughts, which are truly electrical impulses, have a small or significant impact on the entire globe. When we say Vasudeva Kutumbakam, we are stating that we are all members of a larger family known as the world. This family is then subdivided into continents, nations, regions, etc. However, the creator has enacted only one set of universal laws for all of its beings, including the law of gravitation, the law of karma, and the law of attraction, among others. Whether one acknowledges these universal laws or not, they are constantly at work. Likewise, whether one acknowledges it or not, this world is one large family, and we are all members of it.

Yes, it requires maturity, genuine experience, and genuine knowledge to understand this, and most importantly, to embrace everyone as a member of the family. If you can embrace this, then you will only engage in good karmas, you will only have good thoughts for everyone, including your enemies, there will be no conflicts or hostilities based on religion, caste, language, creed, region, etc., and the entire world will be a happy, prosperous, and tranquil family.

Can a particle of the Ocean differ from the Ocean itself?

Does not every ray of the sun emanate from the sun itself? Will the characteristics of a Leaf grown on a Tree differ from those of the Tree?

How can We, who are in actuality Souls originating from the same divine power, be completely dissimilar and unrelated?

It is essential to comprehend who we are, where we originated from, where we will all go after we relinquish our corporeal bodies, and our relationship with God and nature. Our starting point and final destination are the same, but our journeys, experiences, and number of costume changes will vary.

I, this body, am nature (Prakriti), while I, the spirit, am divinity (Purusha). Understanding this difference requires years and years of contemplation, and when we ultimately do, our spiritual journey back to our original home begins in earnest. We reside in Maya (illusion) until then, contending for "I" the body while neglecting "Me" the consciousness.

Few minutes of daily meditation facilitates genuine spiritual awakening, which is the true purpose of I, the soul; all other goals are for the satisfaction of I, the physical body.

If I am not who I believe I am, what am I doing as another person?

Simply ask yourself, "Who am I?" and devote some quality time to finding the answer. Imagine a race without a finish line or pursuing a target without knowing how to get closer to it! Imagine a scenario in which you start your automobile and then drive indefinitely without knowing where you're going or what your destination is. Doesn't it appear absurdly absurd?

However, this is precisely what we are doing right now. We are steering our lives by the seat of our pants without knowing their purpose or destination. First, let's determine who we are; once that is accomplished, our purpose will present itself naturally. Be a good driver of your life, and like a good driver, drive with purpose, observe the universal traffic laws, maintain a healthy body, whistle less, and arrive at your destination on time and without incident.

We are all made from the same White fabric.

Yes, we are the product of the same white cloth cut by the divine hand and then sewn into diversely shaped and colored bodies.

Therefore, we connect emotionally with every living thing on the planet, whether knowingly or unknowingly.

When another person grins, you smile as well. When someone else acquires wealth, you become affluent as well. When someone else is suffering, you experience their anguish as well. It is the same energy that is distributed among all beings and non-beings, as there is only one world and one family. When you assist another person, you also benefit yourself. When you harm another person, you also damage yourself. When you ridicule or abuse another user on Twitter or Facebook, you are also ridiculing yourself. This is why the sayings "what goes around comes around" and "you reap what you sow" exist. It's time to recognize the unity. It is time to explore the interior.

The trillions of cells and thousands of organs in our body obey the commands and instructions of the BRAIN in order to live in harmony as ONE entity.

Similarly, so long as all living and nonliving creatures heed the universal laws and divine scriptures written and amended by HIM, we can all live in harmony as ONE universal Family in this ONE gorgeous world.

Let's extrapolate further: millions of planets, stars, and other celestial entities in millions of galaxies live in harmony, producing the divine sound OM in accordance with specific scientific formulations prescribed by HIM. Therefore, the message is that whether you are a bacterium, a human, a planet, or a galaxy, in order to live in peace, harmony, and the state of Ananda (eternal joy), you must heed certain commands and follow certain instructions from HIM, as everything ultimately converges into a singular entity known as the universe.

How To Meditate

Meditation entails adopting a comfortable posture and bringing your body to a tranquil and mindful state on purpose. Before beginning a meditation session, you must ensure that there will be no interruptions. If necessary, power off your phone or place it in silent mode. If you must inform people that you require a period of peace and silence, then do so.

Choose a location where you feel tranquil and secure. A location with minimal music and mellow illumination can enhance the experience. Relieve your body by using the restroom, consuming a refreshment or meal, and consuming water. This will prevent your physical cravings from distracting you. In addition, you can cleanse your body and moisturize your epidermis. Keeping yourself pleasant can enhance your session experience.

Adjust the temperature of the room or wear appropriate apparel to prevent your body from becoming too heated or chilly. Choose a plush cushion with a comfortable fabric to rest on.

If you intend to use music during your meditation session, choose a familiar piece. This will prevent you from being distracted by unexpected clangs, melodies, or screeches. Keep the music on continuous repeat to prevent you from losing focus to begin a new song.

Meditation position

While there are a variety of meditative postures, including reclining, sitting, moving, and balancing in various positions, many meditation sessions begin and conclude with a simple seated position. Numerous meditation techniques, including deep breathing, imagery, mindfulness, gaze, prayer, and music, can be practiced while seated.

It is essential to maintain a suitable seated position while meditating. It permits excellent circulation and mental acuity while relaxing. It is essential to maintain vigilance so that the session is not merely relaxing but also characterized by mindful awareness.

To begin meditating, you must select a distraction-free space or chamber. The environment's climate must be pleasant. Turn off any electronic device or mobile phone that could be a distraction. Put on clothing that is comfortable. Garments that do not shift, irritate, or press into the sides.

You can recline on an upholstered floor, or if you prefer, you can relax on a sofa, bed, or office bed. Just ensure that your seating arrangement allows you to maintain a strong posture.

Cross your legs in front of you and tilt your sacrum forward to mimic the natural curve of your spine. Spread the weight of your body uniformly between your thighs and buttocks. If seated in a chair, distribute your feet uniformly across the floor.

By elongating your neck and vertebrae, you can align your cranium with your shoulder. Keep your head gently tucked in. Maintain a relaxed mandible, tongue, temples, and eyes. Align the shoulders and the pelvis.

Allow your shoulders to sink back to expand your torso. You could instead extend your legs at the ankles as opposed to crossing them. Gently squeeze the soles of your feet together and nestle your heels close to your pelvis. Lotus, a traditional meditative posture, could be adopted. This involves maintaining crossed legs, with the right foot resting on the left thigh and the left foot on the right thigh.

Rest your arms on your knees or lap with your palms facing either down or up, or loosely cup your hands together. You can form a circle by connecting your index or middle finger to your thumb. This is a traditional hand position for meditation. Then, turn your palms up while resting the backs of your hands on your knees, or turn your hands over to rest on your knees. Nonetheless, if you choose to retain your hands, ensure that your shoulders do not feel strained due to your chosen posture.

Permit your thorax and abdomen to rise and fall naturally as you breathe in and out of your body. Ensure that you are not rigidly seated and allow your shoulders and spine to move with your respiration.

Permit your thorax to expand by taking a few chest-deep breaths. Relax and maintain a sense of an open bosom as you exhale. You are now prepared to begin your meditation exercise.

Meditation techniques

You can incorporate the following uncomplicated modern meditation practices into your daily routine. These practices are suitable for novices and can be performed in any environment. You can practice them in your living room, work cubicle, office, or while sitting next to a river, fountain, or gorgeous garden.

Daily practice of these exercises for as little as ten or fifteen minutes can yield numerous benefits. When you become accustomed to meditation, you can attempt to do them for extended periods. You can engage in this activity for thirty minutes to an hour or longer. Choose one or two activities you believe you might enjoy.

Deep inhalation: If you are new to meditation, you can begin with this practice, as it is the foundation of most meditative practices. You can repeat this process until you feel confident enough to move on to other forms of meditation. Turn off the phones and other distraction-causing devices. Maintain focus on your respiration while maintaining a meditative posture.

Focus on how air fills your lungs and the sounds of your inhalations and exhalations. Keep your respiration steady and profound. If you become diverted and your mind wanders, redirect your attention to the deep breathing exercise. Feel the relief that comes with remaining still and focusing on your respiration. Continue until you experience revitalization and relaxation.

Music for reflection: Choose a site that is free of noise and distractions. You require a location where you can listen to music in comfort. Choose music that interests you and play it. Numerous individuals enjoy using instrumental music, particularly music with noises of chimes, violins, or nature. Assume a seated position and take long breaths. Continue until you reach a state of relaxation. Continue the practice until your mind is devoid of concerns and musings. Focus on the melodies and noises of the music until it has an effect on you. Occasionally, your consciousness will wander. When this occurs, return your focus to the music. Ensure that your respiration is steady and profound.

The Issue Presented By Mindlessness

99.2% of all persons have a wandering consciousness for 99.2% of their waking lives. This is a made-up statistic, but it feels accurate. We all have a mind that wanders almost constantly. We can only observe a film for a few minutes before our minds begin to wander when it is exceedingly captivating. In meditation, we train our consciousness to be able to consistently and for as long as possible focus on our breath. The majority of individuals can only last a few seconds. Over time, however, this focus, concentration, presence, and attentional power become much stronger.

When we lack consciousness, we are unaware of our true nature and desires. We succumb to our primitive instincts and impulses. To satiate our insatiable desire for novelty and increasing stimulation, we are prone to constantly seek out new and novel experiences. This can contribute to a type of wandering eye in city dwellers, as too many options result in too many breakups because we are never satiated. We constantly live in the future, contemplating what comes next. It makes finding commitment considerably more difficult. With today's advanced technology, we have access to an infinite number of options. When we date mindlessly, we float through a multitude of options and people without ever taking the time to determine what we want, who we are, and what we deserve.

Often, mindless courting is based more on chance than on creating opportunities to discover our companion. Mindless courting can feel superficial and unsatisfying. It can even result in remaining with the incorrect person for too long, thereby making it more difficult to find the right one. When we date mindlessly, we are only partially present because we are half (or worse, 90%) in our heads. Therefore, when we date someone, we are truly dating a projection of that person, our interpretation, and we are not completely perceiving them in the present. We do not respect their authentic selves because we see an artificial version of them that resides in our heads. And this is the issue when we are absent from our relationships.

When we are apathetic, we tend to react unconsciously, without the necessary thought and consideration for a suitable response. We may react with fury outbursts, lose our composure, or say things we don't intend if we are reacting unconsciously. When we incorporate mindfulness into our lives and relationships, we create opportunities, shape our lives, and construct our futures. We are not circumstances' victims, but rather conscientious, mindful, and deliberate creators.

The Influence Of Presence

Genuinely talented actors are universally praised for their commanding presence. This is a very suitable term, as what it actually indicates is that they are present. It indicates that they are physically at ease and at ease in the situation. This is the essence of attraction. That is being mindful. Presenteeism is attractive. People gravitate toward those who make them feel at ease. People who feel at ease make others feel at ease. You can unwind around someone who is relaxed, which is why practicing mindfulness is so important if you want to attract a partner.

In standard meditation, we either concentrate on our breath or a mantra as a tool for drawing us into the present moment, to redirect our attention away from thoughts, plans, and the past, and drag us directly into the present. This is because the respiration is always in the present moment. We only concentrate on and experience the respiration in the present moment. We never consider our final breath. We never contemplate our next breath. Only the present breath remains. It is a gateway to the present. Similar to a mantra. The mantra is constantly in the present. Therefore, it transports us into the present.

Over time, something that is performed daily for 10, 20, or 30 minutes becomes a habit and a natural way of life. When this occurs, you attain complete presence. One of the things you learn in acting school is how to release tension from your body, so that when you walk out on stage, you appear as natural, relaxed, and at ease as if 1,000 people weren't watching you. In the same manner, mindfulness and meditation make your natural state of mind relaxed, tranquil, present, aware, vigilant, and focused. You become fully present, aware of your circumstances, aware of yourself, fully confident, fully at peace, and filled with gratitude and pleasure for this sensation and experience.

When you are present, you perceive your surroundings more keenly. You are genuinely open to new opportunities, undiscovered events, and locations to meet new people. When you are completely present, an elevator excursion can become a chance to meet someone. Every location is an opportunity if you are present and open to possibility and chance.

Due to our smartphones, headphones, televisions, and soon-to-be-released virtual reality devices, it is becoming increasingly difficult for us to be present in our modern world. This makes individuals resistant to possibility.

A component of being present is simply being in the present moment and savoring this one, fleeting, full existence we have. It is about being appreciative of each moment and not squandering our precious lives by existing in an imagined or artificial reality, when the actual world is where all the enchantment and profound love and connection exist.

Technology is remarkable for connecting people and allowing us to communicate with distant individuals. However, we are still social creatures who desire physical contact. It is essential to allow for these in-person encounters and meetings. Moreover, because you are not wearing headphones, you may be able to taunt an attractive boy or girl who is wearing headphones for losing out on all the interesting things happening in the present.

Relaxation And Calmness-Inducing Breathing Techniques

Mindful Breathing, as we have seen previously, promotes control over the body and emotions, enhances health, and enables you to make logical decisions. To achieve this state of calm and serenity, you need only to practice. In this chapter, we will examine nine Mindful Breathing techniques that will not only help you understand and quantify your breathing, but also improve your quality of life.

Technique No. 1 for Mindful Breathing: Bee Breathing

First, take a moment to unwind in sukhasana (cross-legged position) with your hands in chin mudra (knowledge mudra).

Perform five seconds of jalandhara bandha (throat contraction) and mule bandha (anal contraction) while taking a long inhalation and filling the lungs with oxygen.

Loosen the bandhas, elevate your arms until they are horizontal at shoulder height, and flex your forearms to cover your ears with your index fingers, ensuring the seal.

Exhale slowly through the nose for approximately 30 seconds while producing a bee-like humming sound. The lips are sealed and the canines are barely separated.

Try to concentrate on the sound and sense the vibration in your cranium. At the conclusion of the exhalation, bring your hands to your knees to finish a round and begin again.

If trained, you can perform between 15 and 20 cycles, but you should begin with 5 and increase progressively. Do not perform this breathwork while reclining down.

What benefits does it provide?

It reduces blood pressure, helps quiet the mind, eliminates anxiety, induces a meditative state, and stimulates the fourth chakra (Anahata).

Diaphragmatic breathing is the second technique for mindful breathing.

Diaphragmatic or abdominal respiration assists diaphragmatic breathing. This is a massive muscle that is essential for respiration. It is located beneath the lungs and divides the thorax from the abdomen.

In the case of chronic pulmonary disease, additional muscles (a combination of chest, shoulder, and neck muscles) may be used instead of the diaphragm. Utilizing these muscles necessitates greater exertion and exacerbates shortness of breath. Using your diaphragm can help you take in more air when you breathe.

The benefits of diaphragmatic respiration include:

Breathe simpler

Inspire more oxygen

Relax Exercise or be more physically active

How does it work?

Place yourself in a comfortable chair or on your back with a bolster beneath your head. Ensure your spine is properly supported.

Place one hand on your sternum and the other on your abdomen, specifically the area above your stomach.

Slowly inhale through your nostrils. I will count to two. Raise your midriff with your hand as you inhale. Your thorax should remain stationary.

Slowly exhale with your lips almost closed together. Count to four. As you exhale, you should feel your midsection deflate.

When inhaling, count to 2 and when exhaling, count to 4. This allows you to maintain calm and constant respiration.

Initially, practice this breathing technique for 5 to 10 minutes. Try to do it three to four times daily. Then, enhance the exercise duration and frequency.

What benefits does it provide?

As you inhale, the diaphragm descends, allowing the lungs to fill with air more completely; as you exhale, the diaphragm returns to its original position. Using the diaphragm to breathe is the correct method to breathe because it increases lung capacity.

Alternate Breathing is the third technique for mindful breathing.

This method is also known as the Anuloma Viloma method. I guarantee that if you practice it, you will rapidly attain calm and mental clarity.

Breathing alternately through each nostril causes a shift from one hemisphere to the other, and this physiological fact gives this relaxation technique tremendous strength.

How do you perform alternate breathing?

Sitting with your back erect, place the thumb of your right hand in the right nostril and the middle or ring finger of your left hand in the left nostril.

To become accustomed to the sensation, seal one nostril at a time. Try to locate a position of satisfaction.

Exhale and inhale on one side, then close that nostril and exhale and exhale on the other side, then close that side again and exhale for the other side for approximately two minutes. "Always starts with exhaling." Slowly and thoroughly inhale the stomach while concentrating on the sensation of air leaving and entering the nostril.

After two minutes, switch hands and repeat the process with the other hand, closing each nostril alternately for another two minutes.

After two minutes, switch to the other hand for a final minute of exercise with her.

Rest both hands for one minute on your knees before continuing with your activities.

What benefits does it provide?

This technique allows air to travel through both nostrils; however, you can observe that one nostril is occluded more than the other throughout the day, and this fluctuates depending on the time of day.

With Anuloma Viloma, you can restore your breathing cycles so that you not only breathe consciously and methodically, but also that your breath becomes consistently thicker, more robust, and more beneficial to your body.

If you cannot sleep at night, try lying on your right side and applying mild pressure to your right nostril pillow while inhaling exclusively through your left nostril. This activates the relaxation and mental tranquility mechanisms that facilitate sleep.

Mindful Breathing Method No. 4: Kapalabhati or Fire Breath

Kapalabhati, also known as fire-spit, is one of the most potent purification techniques in the ancient discipline of Pranayama (breath control techniques associated with the yoga tradition).

The term kapalabhati is translated as "cleansing the skull" or "splendid skull," referring to this exercise's capacity to enhance concentration and interior calm.

How Should You Perform Kapalabhati Breathing?

Choose a peaceful location, free from commotion and environmental contaminants such as dust, pollution or offensive aromas.

Sit in a position of comfort, whether on the floor or in a firm chair. In his book Yoga for the Three Stages, S. Ramaswami explains that the ideal posture for practicing this inhalation is padmasana, or the lotus position. If this pose is not yet available to you, consider Ardha padamasana or half-lotus pose, vajrasana or virasana or hero pose.

Exhale forcefully and forcefully contract the abdominal muscles as you exhale (including through the nose). Pull the abdomen upward with every exhale.

The act of breathing is automatic, but the exhalation must be vigorous and forceful.

For novices, Ramaswami suggests performing kapalabathi in 24-breath intervals with intermediate pauses. Later, it is possible to increase the number of breaths per interval. Three cycles are recommended, possibly followed by other pranayama techniques.

What advantages does it provide?

The following are some of the advantages of this technique:

Purify the airways. This method reduces obstruction in the bronchi and bronchioles progressively. Even in the earliest phases of emphysema, it can aid in restoring normal lung function and restoring the alveoli. Regular exercise helps to cleanse the airways and prevent the development of sinusitis and acute rhinitis, although it is not recommended for those with sinusitis or rhinitis.

Provides allergy and chilly relief. Even with a persistent cough, this ventilation can be advantageous.

Increases metabolic rate and body temperature.

Strengthens the abdominals.

All abdominal organs receive a sufficient massage: the liver, spleen, pancreas, kidneys, adrenal glands, stomach, and intestines all enhance their blood circulation. Consequently, it may be advantageous for individuals with irritable bowel syndrome, constipation, and certain types of diabetes caused by a sluggish pancreas, flatulence, or dyspepsia.

Samavritti Pranayama or "Square Breathing" is the fifth mindful breathing technique.

This inhalation is excellent for unwinding and soothing the psyche. Practicing it will oxygenate your entire body and provide you with additional vitality. The Samavritti Pranayama technique is also beneficial if you have respiratory difficulties or need to expand your rib cage. This exercise strengthens the muscles used for respiration. Follow these straightforward procedures to implement it:

Inhale and count to three while filling the lower portion of your lungs.

Keep your breath for three seconds.

Exhale as you count to three.

Remove air from your lungs for an additional three seconds.

Repeat this cycle without interruption four times.

What benefits does it provide?

When discussing the square, the keyword for this technique is balance - equilibrium of the nervous system, stability of the mind, serenity and peace, as well as the addition of oxygen to the blood and improvement of concentration. Yes, by mentally counting the times, you are not only working on the phases of the respiration, but also on the concentration of the mind, as you lose the thread and break the square when you become distracted.

The Union Of Peace And Understanding

Typically, one achieves tranquility by concentrating on an object. Then, you practice maintaining undistracted concentration on this object. This results in an uninterrupted flow of focus, and your mind becomes extremely stable. The Sadhinirmocana Stra explains that once you have settled into a state of tranquility, you should investigate this state with discernment; this process of analysis is known as insight meditation. In addition, the Mahyna Strlakra states that tranquility is the state of a mind settled in its purity, and an analysis of this state is provided in the Strlakra.This Sadhinirmocana Stra also explains that residing in a state of tranquility is linked to the flexibility of body and mind.d mind. Tranquility and insight without pliability are termed simulated tranquility and insight.The Bodhisattvabhmi explains that once the yogi has attained tranquility, he analyzes the aspects of tThis text explains that while tranquility is a non-conceptual state devoid of dualism, insight recruits discernment to develop wisdom and is therefore a conceptualized percInsight is gained through discrimination that investigates rWhen a practitioner masters tranquility meditation, he or she should engage in insight meditation, which is supported by this very stabThere is a risk that a yogi could become attached to the ecstasy produced by elevated states of concentration.It is believed that familiarity with these states of absorption leads to rebirth in the form and formless. This is an impediment to our liberation, so we should not become attached to the serenity and pleasure of tranquility meditation.Some great mediators who have become intoxicated by the blissful sensation that accompanies intense states of concentration mistake this for absolute reality.In Tibetan, we refer to it as nyentho gokpar, which means everything. all your anguish and distress vanishes When you reach this stage, you are so content and appreciate the flavor of meditation so much that you tend to develop an attachment to it.Eventually, these meditators in profound samdhi will be roused by Buddha's benediction in the form of light, which will emanate onto their bodies to awaken them. The Buddhas will tell them, "Wake up! You still have a long way to go.You are not even resting.These meditators will then follow the bodhisattva path and eventually attain Buddhahood.hahood. While tranquility meditation may temporarily subdue our mental afflictions, insight meditation weakens and ultimately destroys them.We can have many dormant mental afflictions even if we have a very tranquil mind, and we must eliminate them, because if we don't, they will resurface at a later date and cause us to suffer.The treatment for these issues is insight mediMeditation is the instrument with which we can eliminate these mental obscurities.ations. Tranquility without insight temporarily suppresses our mental afflictions, but it is the wisdom that stems from insight and is sustained by tranquility that will eradicate our delusion.This is explicitly declared in the Sadhinirmocan.a Stra, so both tranquility and insight are required to achieve realization.Eventually, both forms of meditation will converge, like several rivers streaming in opposite directions merging into a single ocean; when this occurs, we will achieve realiThis is the union of tranquility and perception, amath and vipayan. The two disciplines of tranquility and insight meditation must be combined, which is feasible because they are identical in terms of their goals. They are similar to a single entity with two distinct aspects.Someone may believe that the union of tranquility and insight is impossible because they perceive tranquility to be non-conceptual and insight to be conceptual.eptual. However, their union is feasible because even during tranquility meditation on the visualized object of the Buddha, for instance, there is discernment because we know it to be the form of the Buddha. Buddha. Furthermore, flawless insight is regarded as non-concThus, there is no contradiction between tranquility and irrationality.Combining tranquility and insight is like gluing two poles together. If you touch the two poles together for a long time, you will create a spark. After starting a fire, even the twigs will ignite and be consumed by the flames. It is possible to have tranquility toward an object, a condition of concentration that does not abandon the object, while simultaneously analyzing the actuality of that object. In this fashion, the two facets of tranquility and insight are merged.arable.

Meditation Practice Everyday

In the previous chapter, we examined the finest meditational practices for you to attempt, and in this chapter, you will learn how to make meditation a permanent habit. Occasionally, it may be necessary to plan your meditational practice in order to help it stay. This can be accomplished by following the procedures listed below.

Adopt a schedule

Always adhere to a schedule when it comes to meditation practice. You must establish a daily time and location and arrive there on time every day. You can maintain a reminder on your phone or download an app that prompts you to meditate periodically. You can also ask a family member to remind you, just in case you forget. During the first few days, forgetfulness will be pervasive; therefore, it will be crucial for you to remember and meditate on time every day.

Prepare yourself

The next step is to prepare yourself by purchasing all necessary supplies. Even though meditation can be practiced anywhere, it is best to adhere to the prescribed method. To be completely prepared, you can purchase a mat (yoga mat will suffice), some tranquil music CDs, a few aromatherapy lamps, and a photograph of a calming scene, such as a landscape or Buddha. If you believe you will need additional items, you may purchase them, but be careful not to spend too much money and purchase only the absolute necessities.

Discipline

Next, you must comprehend that you must possess a great deal of discipline. You cannot approach meditation with a casual attitude; you must resolve to devote yourself completely to the practice. You must never take it casually and exert maximum effort to ensure that the habit sticks.

Atmosphere

Always create the ideal environment when performing yoga. You cannot recline anywhere you please and expect to be able to engage in tranquil meditation.

You must first locate a secluded area where no one and no noise are present. If the environment is boisterous, then your mind will wander and you will be unable to meditate in tranquility.

The air in the room should be the next consideration. The air must be spotless, purified, and devoid of pollution. You can rest in your garden or another area with abundant vegetation. Additionally, you can maintain plants in your bedroom or living room.

Thirdly, you must play calming music in the backdrop. This music must be soothing, and it can be the sound of a waterfall, birds tweeting, or any form of soothing classical music.

Lastly, you must ensure that aromatherapy candles are lit to enhance your experience. Lavender, rose, and sandalwood are some of the finest aromas to help you unwind. If you do not have candles, you can also use incense sticks.

Disconnect

When you settle down to meditate, you must eliminate all potential distractions. Before you set down to meditate, you must ensure that your cell phone is turned off and stored away, as it is one of the primary distractions. Additionally, you must turn off the television and any other similar distractions. If necessary, you can pass your phone to another person and ask them to answer your calls. Before you settle down, you must check for any other potential distractions, such as an open flame in the kitchen or anything else that could be turned on or off, lest you have to get up in the midst of your practice.

Seating

When it comes to accommodation, sitting on the ground with no lumbar support is optimal. This causes the entire back and spinal cord to lengthen. If you are unable to do so, you can recline on a chair with a high back.

You may also rest on a sofa or bed, so long as they do not make you drowsy, and it is recommended that you do not recline, unless you are using the visualization technique.

Progress

A progress summary is one of the best methods to keep track of your routine and remain motivated. You can write down everything you believe to be wrong with you at the start of your meditation practice and then re-record it every few days to track the progress. You must remember to keep the record and not let it slip your mind. You must keep a journal or record your thoughts in a digital format on your smartphone, tablet, or computer. Additionally, never compare your development to that of others. Sometimes you may be in the lead and sometimes they may be, but you must always maintain your position.

Partner

Taking up the practice with a companion is a good method to remain still. Your partner can be your spouse, life partner, closest friend, brother, sister, or mother, among other possibilities. Anyone interested in meditating and reaping its benefits would make an excellent companion. One of the greatest benefits of having a companion is that the two of you will keep each other motivated and refuse to stop practicing.

Expectations

It is essential that you have reasonable expectations when it comes to this. If your expectations are unreasonable, you will undoubtedly be disappointed. When starting out, it is essential to recognize that you will not be able to levitate or become the wealthiest individual. Meditation is a form of discipline-inducing practice, without a doubt, but it has its own limitations. You must also have reasonable expectations regarding how long it will take to see results, which can range from one week to one month depending on your level of commitment.

Never quit!

Finally, you should never quit. Once you begin meditating, you must practice it consistently until it becomes a permanent habit. It is not something that can be undertaken quickly and abandoned readily. You must adopt a new lifestyle and adhere to it permanently.

Transcendental Meditation

A practitioner of transcendental meditation rests for 20 minutes, twice daily, using a nonverbal sound or mantra to achieve a state of profound tranquility. In the mid-1950s, Maharishi Mahesh Yogi created it. Even though its origins are in Hinduism, a practitioner is not required to be Hindu or to profess any faith to practice yoga.

Beginners in TM work one-on-one with an instructor for an initial period. Ideally, the instructor is a seasoned practitioner who has been instructed to instruct and provide students with any necessary follow-up. Good instructors tailor their methods to each individual student.

The initial instruction consists of seven steps: two lectures and an interview, followed by four days of individual sessions. Each session should last approximately one and a half hours.

Following these seven stages, the student will check in with the instructor at predetermined intervals, typically weekly for the first four weeks and then monthly thereafter. Students are able to ask inquiries and ensure their technique is accurate during these meetings.

Benefits of Transcendental Meditation to Health

One of the most researched types of meditation, transcendental meditation has been shown to provide the following health benefits:

Increase longevity

Reduce the incidence of metabolic syndrome

Teens with elevated blood pressure should lower their blood pressure.

Reduce the enlargement of coronary arteries

Reduce arterial plaque

Control or prevent stress

Reduce myocardial infarction.

Adjusting cholesterol levels

Treat epilepsy

Contribute to smoking cessation

Practice

Because TM employs a mantra, it is considered a form of concentration practice, although the goal is not focused attention but rather the ability to be receptive to everything around you and pay attention to it. Numerous practitioners believe that TM is a natural process through which the body achieves uncomplicated relaxation, spontaneous imagery, and emotion.

In transcendental meditation, practitioners are instructed to focus on their mantra and not their errant thoughts.

There are between four and ten million transcendental meditation practitioners in the globe.

Mantra

The fundamental technique of this form of meditation is to discreetly and effortlessly repeat your mantra. No specific seated position is required, but the eyes should be closed. The mantra is what enables the practitioner's focus to shift to a peaceful, more tranquil realm. To ensure maximal effectiveness, the mantra must remain a secret.

Individuals choose mantras based on their age and gender. Many TM adherents assert that using the incorrect mantra is hazardous. The sounds come from the Vedic tradition and have no particular significance. They are valuable solely for their music. When someone uses a TM mantra, they are not contemplating on the sound or its significance; rather, they are using the sound to guide their mind to a state of calm.

The Transcendental Meditation Group.

The policies and practices of the TMO, or Transcendental Meditation Organization, are highly controversial. It is possible to spend a substantial quantity of money attending more and more courses to advance one's education. Some dissatisfied practitioners assert that only their wallets became lighter.

It is possible to receive training in transcendental meditation and then continue practicing on one's own, thereby avoiding the controversy of the parent organization.

TM and Studies

Early research on Transcendental Meditation (TM) focused on the physiological effects of meditation, while later research examined cognitive effects, medical costs, mental health benefits, and rehabilitation. In the 1990s, researchers shifted their focus to the cardiovascular impacts of TM. In all fields, additional independent research must be conducted to confirm the results of previous, not always independent studies.

Comparing Transcendental Meditation to Other Faiths

The majority of people describe TM as a simple, nearly effortless method of meditation suitable for people of all faiths. The mantras are merely meaningless sounds, and the practice does not invoke any deities. Some Christian religious leaders believe it is compatible with their faith, while others disagree. Some Jewish rabbis have stated that it is compatible with Judaism, while others have stated that it is not.

If you are concerned about this, consult your spiritual leader and make your own decision.

Unlike many other religions, transcendental meditation has no code of ethics, no public worship, no rites of passage, no scriptures, dietary laws, or pilgrimages.

Brain and Transcendental Meditation

It has been demonstrated that regular transcendental meditation increases the coherence of brain waves. This means that the various regions of the brain function in greater harmony during and after meditation. Electroencephalograms (EEGs) have demonstrated that TM impacts the prefrontal hemispheres of the brain, resulting in enhanced concentration, decision-making, and job performance.

On a piece of paper (of any size), list the objectives you've been endeavoring to attain, i.e., the ones you believe will bring you happiness. For instance, a new job, a home in a pleasant neighborhood, traversing the world, a business, a family, new friends, a degree or certification, building a network, accumulating a million-dollar net worth, etc.

Now, rip the paper into several fragments and discard.

If not obsessively pursued, goals can be extremely useful and beneficial. In the modern world, however, individuals develop a dependence on objectives. Consider all the times you've said, "I must obtain that," "I must achieve that," "I'll do anything to achieve that," etc. Frequently, people spend more time fretting about their objectives than doing something spontaneously in the present to achieve them. In addition, the destination is ephemeral, whereas the voyage in the present moment is genuine and enduring.

Associations subtly inculcate the mentality that objectives must be attained or else failure will ensue. Does the meaning of the word "I" alter depending on whether you have experienced defeat or success? What does it mean to say "I am a failure" or "I am a success"? Exists "I" independent of failure and success? Does "I" exist apart from goals?

*Ten minutes of silence and deliberate respiration. Repetition of the mantra: "Achieving an objective does not affect my contentment. I am now content. I am."

(Share this experience with the hashtag #30DaysGoals)

Day 10

Exercise:

Imagine the following: It is 3:00 AM currently. You awaken to discover that your house is on fire. Except for yourself, everyone has left the premises. You recognize that you have less than a minute to escape before everything is obliterated. You must take urgent action.

What do you gather to bring with you in such a limited quantity of time?

Consider this scenario carefully, as it occurs every day somewhere in the world. People are compelled to abandon their residences due to fire, flooding, violence, and other uncontrollable circumstances. What physical items would you grasp and take in such a brief period of time if this were to occur? Your cell phone, family photographs, computer, passport, money, particular files, a project, or nothing? Whatever you choose in that instant will be the most significant items for you. What does this reveal about your desires, attachments, worries, needs, and routines?

As previously stated, our illusion of "I" is associated with many external factors. Self-observation is the key to discovering the genuine "I" as previously stated. What would be the most essential item for you to save if your home caught fire? This is not to imply that what you ingest has a negative association; rather, it is meant to assist you observe what is associated with your sense of self.

*Ten minutes of silence and deliberate respiration. Mantra: "I am not my possessions." I am unencumbered by anything. I am merely"

A BASIC MEDITATION FOR BEGINNERS

The first thing to explain is that what we're doing here is not a magical method for clearing your mind clean of the innumerable and infinite erupted and pinging in our neurons. We only practice bringing our attention to our respiration and returning to it when we notice that it has wandered.

Make yourself comfortable and prepare to silently sit for a few minutes. After you finish perusing this, you will only be able to concentrate on your natural inhalation and exhalation.

Concentrate on the exhalation. Where are you most aware of your breath? In your belly? In your nose? Maintain your focus on inhaling and exhaling.

Observe your breathing for two minutes. Take a deep breath in, allow your stomach to expand, and then exhale slowly, elongating the exhalation as your stomach contracts.

We "practice" consciousness so that we can learn to recognize when our minds are straying from their normal daily activities and to take a brief break from that so that we can choose what we wish to concentrate on.

If you are experiencing interference, which everyone does, you have made an important discovery: interference is the polar antithesis of consciousness. It is when we exist in our heads, on autopilot, allowing our minds to wander and explore, for example, the future or the past, and were not present at the time. But if we're being honest, that's where the majority of us spend most of our time and where we feel most at home, right? But it does not have to like it.

We "practice" so that we can learn to recognize when our minds are straying from their normal daily activities and to take a brief break so we can choose what we wish to concentrate on. Meditation enables us to have a healthier relationship with ourselves (and, by extension, with others).

WHY LEARN TO MEDITATE?

When we meditate, we imbue our lives with far-reaching and long-lasting benefits. And as an added benefit, you need neither additional equipment nor valuable allies.

Here are five advantages of meditation:

Understand your suffering

2: Reduce your tension level 3: Improve your relationships

Improve concentration and reduce mental distractions

HOW TO MEDITATE

Meditation is simpler (and more difficult) than the majority of people believe. Read these steps, ensure that you're in a place where you can unwind during the process, set a timer, and try it out.

- TAKE A SEAT

Find opinions that are still and silent.

Establish a time limit

Choose a small amount of time, such as 5 or 10 minutes, if you are just beginning.

TAKE NOTICE OF YOUR BODY

You can rest in a chair with your feet on the ground, or you can sit loosely with your legs crossed. You can kneel without issue. Ensure that you are stable and in a position where you can remain for some time.

SENSE YOUR BREATHING

Follow the sensation of your respiration while walking, and he exited the building.

• NOTICE WHEN YOUR MIND HAS WANDERED

Eventually, attention will abandon a pause and move to other locations. When you realize that your mind has wandered - in a few seconds, minutes, or five minutes - simply return your focus to your breathing.

BE KIND TO YOUR WANDERING THOUGHTS

Do not evaluate yourself or become preoccupied with the content of your thoughts. To simply return.

• CLOSE WITH KINDNESS

When ready, raise your gaze gently; if your eyes are closed, uncover them. Take a pause to listen to the sounds around you. Observe how your body currently feels. Consider your thoughts and feelings.

That is all! That is the custom. You leave, you return, and you attempt to do so as compassionately as possible.

Including A Mantra In One's Breathing

Breathing is the foundation for all subsequent exercises in meditation. As previously discussed, you should devote your initial sessions to refining your techniques for soothing your body, mind, and spirit through focused breathing. This will enable you to enter a contemplative state in which you can embrace the restorative benefits of all subsequent meditation. Once you have enabled your mind to be at peace through breathing, you can spend less time per session on simple breathing exercises and progress on to more complex tools that will bring you a deeper understanding of your body while emphasizing pleasure and serenity.

There may be complete silence, background noise, or calm repetitive sounds such as flowing water or soothing music at the location of your exercises. Our mind is prepared for acceptance of this meditative state by a soothing sound. On a subconscious level, music can enlighten our spirits and open our hearts to tranquility. As the gentle music plays, it flows over us, releasing our tensions and infusing our psyche with the tranquility required for inner serenity.

A Mantra, also known as chanting, serves as a substitute for background music. It aids in the creation of the environment necessary to achieve the contentment and serenity you seek through meditation. A mantra is a specific word or phrase that is repeated until the mind is focused on nothing but that word or phrase, blotting out any other distracting noises or events. The word or phrase can be anything, so long as you can readily recall it during each session. Mantra translates to "instrument of your mind" in Sanskrit.

This instrument can be crucial to achieving the desired interior tranquility.

There are many excellent words and phrases from which to choose, but novices may wish to select words that have a double meaning, such as serenity, tranquility, solitude, calm, and similar terms. This will induce the beneficial effects of meditation while focusing your thoughts on the concepts you wish to achieve.

Some proponents of meditation believe chanting induces certain mental vibrations. These vibrations permit the mind to dispel external thoughts and concentrate on the mantra in order to enter a more reflective state of consciousness. It may be stereotypical, but "ummmm" or "mmm" is a common incantation or mantra in many sessions. This is said to be a positive vibration that your body can produce, allowing your mind to absorb the soul's energy as you chant "ummm."

As you breathe in and out, you should mentally repeat the mantra over and over again. Let the word or phrase percolate through your mind by repeating it and concentrating on it. The word itself is more essential than its meaning. Focus your attention on the act of reciting the word or phrase. As you become increasingly contemplative, it may no longer be necessary to recite the word or phrase. However, this is only possible once you have mastered your technique.

As with designating periods for breathing exercises, you should establish a specific duration for chanting your chosen phrase. You can begin with a brief period of time, say five minutes, and gradually increase the length of your sessions by mentally repeating your mantra. By focusing on your word or phrase, your concentration will increase, allowing you to focus your mind, eradicate distractions, and allow positive energy to circulate through your body.

This should not be an automated recital. You may sense yourself drifting away from the session as a novice. If this occurs, merely refocus your attention on the word and the chanting itself. You will eventually reach a point where the chanting becomes secondary to your pleasure and delight.

Our Programming

On the path to maturity and becoming an adult, everyone has been programmed towards something. The programming process occurs without your knowledge. It originates from various sources, including peers and parents, television and textbooks, the government and the church, Hollywood and Madison Avenue, and so on.

All the influences to which you are exposed have an impact on you, and they imprint perspectives, ideas, aspirations, outlooks, expectations, and desires on a mind that is already susceptible to influence. You grow up as the slave of a programmed mind.

The program will determine how you react to various life situations and how you behave in general. Deliberate deprogramming is the only means of liberation from such conditioning. Most things require that you query, ponder, and analyze them.

As you query and examine the things you have accepted, you are able to distinguish between what is true and what is deceptive; you can distinguish between what is good and what is evil, as well as reality and illusion.

The deprogramming process will continue throughout your life, but there will be times when it is more intense than others. As you ponder, query, and pursue the truth, you develop your own opinions and biases. When this occurs, the biases, opinions, and philosophies you acquire will filter and screen every idea from the outside and every perspective and viewpoint your mind encounters.

As a result, you become receptive to some ideas while unable to receive others; those that your mind cannot receive ricochet off and leave no impression. Since you know the truth, your mind becomes less impressionable and malleable; it stops worrying about error and simply disregards it.

The programming of the mind will not proceed without your intervention. Reason, your current philosophies, your conscience, and your outlook will influence the final outcome. Keep in mind that some of the most commonly presumed notions stem from societal and individual implicit assumptions. This is the programming that will pass unchecked by the conscience and the consciousness.

In this chapter, you will gain an understanding of the law of cause and effect, how it interacts with the physical world, and how to begin deprogramming your mind.

The universal law of consequence and cause

According to the universal law of cause and effect, each effect has a distinct cause, and each cause has a distinct effect. Your behaviors, beliefs, and actions will have consequences that will manifest as your life.

Consequently, if you are dissatisfied with the effects or your beliefs, you must alter their causes. To alter your life and behavior, you must alter your beliefs; in this way, you can create a different future.

The law of cause and effect cannot be altered. You will not only learn about it as an unattainable phenomenon, but also as something you can use to enhance your life. The premise is that existence is not the result of accidents, chance, or fate. You will also learn the dynamics of choice in order to comprehend the ways in which you choose unconsciously or consciously your daily experiences and emotions. You will discover some queries that will assist you in your analysis and pursuit of this universal law.

It would be challenging to discuss the law of cause and effect without mentioning the law of attraction.

While this section will not delve thoroughly into the law of attraction, it is important to note that among other laws, the law of cause and effect serves as its foundation. By grasping these laws, you can use the law of attraction to achieve your life's deepest desires. Remember that the law of attraction has been misrepresented and promoted as a shortcut to a successful life by many people, but that is not its purpose.

As stated previously, the law of cause and effect states that every effect has a specific and predictable cause, and every action has a specific and predictable effect.

Everything you are presently experiencing in life is an effect that resulted from a cause. The causes could be your daily actions or the choices you make. Regardless of the magnitude of these decisions, they have consequences; it makes no difference whether the choice appears transformative or inconsequential.

Every choice you've made and action you've taken has initiated events and generated predictable consequences that you must now manage.

The statute goes on to specify that:

Success in any endeavor or field will result directly from specific actions and causes.

Success in any endeavor is the indirect result of particular actions and causes.

Simply stated, attaining any degree of success in anything you do is predictable and repeatable if you are mindful of your actions. This essentially means that if you make the right decisions and do the right things, you will achieve the success you desire, whether you are certain of it or not.

Consequently, the law emphasizes the notion that achieving achievement is straightforward if you know what you want. All that is required is knowledge of the decisions and actions of successful individuals that led to their success.

After determining their actions, you must identify their choices, beliefs, habits, values, emotions, psychological norms and meta-programs, and behaviors.

This essentially implies that you must observe successful individuals. Using the law of cause and effect, you can attract similar success and outcomes to yourself once you've gained an understanding of how they operate in various domains.

There Are No Mishaps.

According to the law, success is not the result of fate or coincidence, nor is it determined by external factors; rather, it is something that you create within yourself.

According to the law, nothing in this world is a coincidence, and the effects you create in your life are the consequence of your own actions. The law explains further that whatever occurs, whether evil or beneficial, occurs for a reason.

Since nothing is the product of fate or accident, everything that occurs is the result of your own actions. Then, life does not have favorites. You attract into your life things that are a direct result of you; you create these things.

Moreover, the law states that the circumstances of your life will have varying effects. The reactions you have to people and events will determine your behavior and your emotions.

You have control over who you have been over time, who you will be tomorrow, and the current and future circumstances and conditions of your existence. In fact, how you respond to people, situations, and events right now determines how you will feel every day. It is producing effects that transform your fate daily.

The law also discusses the potency of thought.

Your thoughts are capable of forming causes. They attribute significance to various situations and manifest your reality. Thus, what you encounter in life is a reflection of your beliefs.

Within each of your thoughts are the causes that have the ability to manifest your reality. The causes produce effects that you experience throughout your existence as the circumstances you encounter.

Your opinions are expansive. They give significance to how you experience reality, which explains why you have the perspective you do on the world.

You have a sovereign will

Your ability to regulate your beliefs is the only thing you have control over from the moment you enter this world.

According to the law, you are free to interpret your experiences as you see fit. At any given time, you can choose to experience emotions both subconsciously and consciously. You also choose your actions based on how you perceive the world, yourself, others, and events.

Since you always have the option to control your thoughts and since your thoughts can generate the causes and effects you experience in life, it follows that you have chosen the life you are living, whether or not you realize it.

Further, the law states that the choice you've always had has shaped your learned behaviors, thoughts, responses, interpretations, and reactions to life and circumstances. You experience life as you do due to conditioned and learned patterns that were programmed into your consciousness over the course of a life in which you had free will.

As discussed previously, the programming filters the way you experience reality in a biased and predictable manner, creating and interpreting your existence. The law then offers a solution to the problem by stating that since you have free will, you can choose to alter your thoughts, actions, and behaviors.

As a thinker, you can choose to be cognizant and proactive due to your freedom of choice.

The freedom of choice suggests that it is never too late to make a desired change.

Regardless of how unfavorable your circumstances are, how 'unlucky' you believe you are, or how bleak your experiences, having a choice implies that you can choose differently. You can unlearn the things you've learned, which will result in causes that have positive effects and alter your existence.

Analysis queries

The law of cause and effect has provided you with numerous guiding principles. They can help determine your future course of action. Here you will find queries that will assist you in applying the universal law, as opposed to allowing it to govern your behavior unconsciously.

The queries are intended to provide insight into your thought processes and life, allowing you to find the answers that will help you achieve your desired level of success. Answer them truthfully and take the time to reflect:

How do my beliefs create and sustain the life I am currently living?

How can I begin to perceive the universe differently?

How do I alter my manner of thinking?

In what ways should I emulate the successful behaviors, decisions, thoughts, and actions of others?

The underlying principles of the law of cause and effect are profound and profound. They enable you to view existence as more than a series of arbitrary events. You view life as something you can predict and exert control over in order to shape and create a daily experience you enjoy.

www.ingramcontent.com/pod-product-compliance
Lightning Source LLC
Chambersburg PA
CBHW050243120526
44590CB00016B/2196